SHAKIN' THE MESS OUTTA MISERY

A Play
by
SHAY YOUNGBLOOD

Dramatic Publishing
Woodstock, Illinois • London, England • Melbourne, Australia

*** NOTICE ***

The amateur and stock acting rights to this work are controlled exclusively by THE DRAMATIC PUBLISHING COMPANY without whose permission in writing no performance of it may be given. Royalty fees are given in our current catalogue and are subject to change without notice. Royalty must be paid every time a play is performed whether or not it is presented for profit and whether or not admission is charged. A play is performed anytime it is acted before an audience. All inquiries concerning amateur and stock rights should be addressed to:

DRAMATIC PUBLISHING
P. O. Box 129, Woodstock, Illinois 60098.

COPYRIGHT LAW GIVES THE AUTHOR OR THE AUTHOR'S AGENT THE EXCLUSIVE RIGHT TO MAKE COPIES. This law provides authors with a fair return for their creative efforts. Authors earn their living from the royalties they receive from book sales and from the performance of their work. Conscientious observance of copyright law is not only ethical, it encourages authors to continue their creative work. This work is fully protected by copyright. No alterations, deletions or substitutions may be made in the work without the prior written consent of the publisher. No part of this work may be reproduced or transmitted in any form or by any means, electronic or mechanical, including photocopy, recording, videotape, film, or any information storage and retrieval system, without permission in writing from the publisher. It may not be performed either by professionals or amateurs without payment of royalty. All rights, including but not limited to the professional, motion picture, radio, television, videotape, foreign language, tabloid, recitation, lecturing, publication, and reading are reserved. *On all programs this notice should appear:*

"Produced by special arrangement with
THE DRAMATIC PUBLISHING COMPANY of Woodstock, Illinois"

©MCMXCIV by
SHAY YOUNGBLOOD

Printed in the United States of America
All Rights Reserved
(SHAKIN' THE MESS OUTTA MISERY)

*Cover photograph by Greg Saylor
Used by permission. All rights reserved.*

Cover design by Susan Carle

ISBN 0-87129-297-1

To all my Big Mamas now living
and those whose spirits have passed on.

SHAKIN' THE MESS OUTTA MISERY was first presented by Horizon's Theatre Company in a workshop production at Spelman College in Atlanta, Georgia in July 1988 directed by Elizabeth Omilami.

The play premiered in Atlanta at Horizon's Theatre Company in Octorber 1988. Set Design by Tom Brown, Lighting by Liz Lee, Costumes by Yvonne Lee, Music by Valetta Anderson. Glenda Dickerson directed the following cast:

Daughter	*Marguerite Hannah*
Big Mama	*Georgia Allen*
Aunt Mae	*Ginnie Randall*
Fannie Mae	*Valarie Eileen Henry*
Miss Corine/Miss Tom	*Mary Holloway*
Miss Mary/Miss Shine	*Carol Mitchell-Leon*
Maggie/Dee Dee	*Margo Williams Moorer*
Miss Lamama	*Elizabeth Omilami*

Acknowledgments

SHAKIN' THE MESS OUTTA MISERY benefitted richly from the editing and dramaturgical advice provided by Gayle Austin, Isabelle Bagshaw and Glenda Dickerson.

Special thanks to Isabelle Bagshaw for her listening ear and loving support.

SHAKIN' THE MESS OUTTA MISERY

A Play in Two Acts
For Eight Women, doubling

CHARACTERS

DAUGHTER . . . . black woman, mid to late 20s
(acts as a child in scenes and as narrator)

*Most other main characters are black women
aged fifty plus and have Southern accents.*

BIG MAMA . . . . Daughter's guardian
AUNT MAE . . . . Big Mama's sister
MISS CORINE . . . . a hair dresser and professional maid
MAGGIE . . . . a con woman
(also plays Dee Dee and Miss Rosa)
MISS MARY . . . . a maid with unearthly powers
(also plays Miss Tom)
MISS TOM . . . . a carpenter and Prayer Circle member
(also plays Miss Mary)
MISS LAMAMA . . a maid with an African husband and ways
DEE DEE . . . . Daughter's fast cousin and know-it-all
(also plays Miss Rosa and Maggie)
YOUNG WOMAN . . . . on bus as maid [no dialog]
(also plays Fannie Mae and Miss Shine)

MISS ROSA . . . . runs funeral home
(also plays Dee Dee and Maggie)
FANNIE MAE . . . . Daughter's blood Mama, a dancing ghost
(also plays Young Woman)
MISS SHINE . . . . a maid at governor's mansion
(also plays Fannie Mae)

Doubling of characters can be reassigned except Big Mama,
Daughter and Fannie Mae.

Additional character notes in back of script.

TIME:
1920s to present.

PLACE:
A small southern town;
a place where memories and dreams coincide.

ACT ONE

AT RISE: *DAUGHTER enters wearing a black coat and hat. She removes her hat and walks around set humming, touching things in a familiar way, remembering, i.e., at Aunt Mae's table, she pretends to pour a drink and toast, at vanity she brushes her hair in mirror, hesitantly sits in Big Mama's rocker, closes her eyes and eases into a story.*

DAUGHTER. I was raised in this house by some of the wisest women to see the light of day. They're all gone now. I buried the last one today. Seems like yesterday they was sitting around in this room talking about taking me to the river. I guess they waited to see me steady on my feet before leaving. Those old snuff dippers taught me some things about living and loving and being a woman. I miss hugging them. *(Hugs herself.)* Wrapped up in the warmth of their love, I listened to them all through the years of my childhood, spellbound by their stories of black women surviving with dignity. Big Mama raised me mostly. I didn't call her Big Mama 'cause she was big or even 'cause she was my mama, she wasn't either. She was just regular. An old black woman who had a gift for seeing with her heart. *(DAUGHTER stands and removes her coat. She is wearing a simple pastel summer dress.)*

(The WOMEN enter humming, forming a circle around the perimeters of the space. DAUGHTER is center stage. Dur-

ing their intro each WOMAN exchanges places with DAUGHTER in center. WOMEN sing African ritual song to Yemenjah, Yoruba river orisha to accept their gifts and answer their prayers. "Yemenjah, Yemenjah olodo, Yemenjah ee ah mee olodo." Repeat one time.)

BIG MAMA. Eyes don't see everything only God can do that.

DAUGHTER. Aunt Mae was Big Mama's sister. She taught me how to wear a tall hat on a windy day and how to walk in high heel shoes. She ran an after hours liquor business out of her kitchen. She was what you'd call an independent woman.

AUNT MAE. The wine taste sweeter and the berries have more juice when you got your own.

DAUGHTER. And I'll never forget Miss Mary. She knew how to work roots and fix people. Sometimes in the middle of a conversation she would see into your future and start to tell it to you if you didn't stop her.

MISS MARY. I ain't never fixed nobody didn't need it.

DAUGHTER. Miss Corine was one of my best friends. Friday and Saturday evenings she ran a beauty shop outta her kitchen. She had Indian blood in her and was quick to admit to Geechees on her daddy's side. That's why folks said she had fingers that could braid the wind.

MISS CORINE. You got to know where you come from to know where you going.

DAUGHTER. Ooh, and Miss Lamama. Her real name was Jessie Pearl Lumumba. When she was seventeen she married an African and took to wearing African dresses and took on African-like ways. That marriage I heard lasted till Mr. Lumumba brought up the possibility of wife number two.

MISS LAMAMA. What don't kill you, will make you strong.

DAUGHTER. The summer I was twelve I was at a bend in the road and it was scary not knowing what was on the other side. My blood mama Fannie Mae wasn't there anymore and my Big Mamas kept talking about taking me to the river, a strange and mysterious place.

BIG MAMA. Daughter got her blood this morning. We gonna have to take her to the river.

MISS MARY. I could have told you that. I seen the signs.

AUNT MAE. Looks like time done sneaked up on us. She's becoming a woman. We got to keep a sharp eye on her.

MISS CORINE. By the time her mama come to us she was already on the road to ruin.

MISS LAMAMA. Daughter been restless, asking lots of questions.

MISS CORINE. It's about time she got some answers.

ALL WOMEN. Her gifts too.

BIG MAMA. We can give her what we couldn't give her mama. *(WOMEN sing: "Yemenjah, Yemenjah olodo, Yemenjah ee ah mee olodo." Repeat one time.)*

ALL WOMEN. Yes.

BIG MAMA. Now, Daughter, on your birthday we gonna take you to the river.

DAUGHTER *(insolent)*. Why I have to go now?

BIG MAMA. Your blood's come. There are some things you need to know and going to the river is a thing you need to do.

DAUGHTER. It's a long way to the river.

BIG MAMA. Don't have to be no river there.

DAUGHTER. Well, what happens at the river?

BIG MAMA. When a girl child get her first blood...

MISS LAMAMA. Her mama or one like her mama have to prepare her.

AUNT MAE. Tell her things a woman needs to know.

MISS MARY. Then the women in the family can take her to a secret place for the crossing over.

BIG MAMA. All summer long your Big Mamas gonna be getting you ready.

ALL WOMEN. Your Big Mamas gonna get you ready.

DAUGHTER. There were so many women and so much love, but something was missing. It was my mama. Fannie Mae wasn't really around anymore, not for real, but I could talk to her, and I would ask her about things. Sometimes I'd even talk to God like Big Mama did. "Dear God, please bless Fannie Mae, Big Mama, Aunt Mae, Miss Corine, Miss Tom, Miss Mary, Miss Rosa and anybody else I forgot. If you have time bless my cousin Dee Dee, even if she is mean to me, I'll need somebody to play with in heaven. And God, I been praying for this last thing a long time now and I hope you hearing me, could you please send my mama back. I miss her. I need her to take me to the river. Amen." Mama? Mama, they want to take me to the river, but I told them I don't wanna go. Well, Dee Dee went two years ago and she mean as ever. Mama, I need you...Why did you leave me?

BIG MAMA. Who you in there talking to?

DAUGHTER. I was thinking, Big Mama.

BIG MAMA. Chile, you suppose to be asleep by now. What you thinking so hard about?

DAUGHTER. About dying.

BIG MAMA. You too young to be thinking 'bout dying, sugar.

DAUGHTER. Not me, Big Mama. I'm scared you might die, then what I do?

BIG MAMA. I ain't goin' nowhere till the Lord is ready for me. Listen, baby, your Big Mama got a whole lot more livin' to do.

Act I   SHAKIN' THE MESS OUTTA MISERY   Page 11

DAUGHTER. You not gonna go away like my mama did?

BIG MAMA. I ain't goin' nowhere you can't reach me by calling my name. You my sugarfoot and I wouldn't choose to leave you for all the angels in heaven. Stop worrying unnecessary. You got all your Big Mamas. We all gonna be getting you ready. Now you go on to sleep and don't forget to say your prayers.

DAUGHTER. Yes ma'am. Things be going bad for Big Mama, she would up and go to the Bible. She had faith in the power of The Man above to work miracles, and me, I had faith in Big Mama.

SCENE TWO

DAUGHTER. Colored folks as you know are the most amazing people on this earth. Big Mama raised me in the company of wise old black women like herself who managed to survive some dangerous and terrible times and live to tell about them. Their only admitted vice, aside from exchanging a little bit of no-harm-done gossip now and then, was dipping snuff. They were always sending me to Mr. Joe's grocery store to buy silver tins of the fine brown powder wrapped in bright colored labels with names like Bruton's Sweet Snuff, Georgia Peach and Three Brown Monkies. One time, my mean old cousin Dee Dee told me that snuff was really ground up monkey dust, a delicacy in the royal palaces of Africa.

(DEE DEE enters with straw in a cup. DAUGHTER skips over to her, curious. They begin hand clapping game, singsong their responses.)

DEE DEE. For real, girl! I ain't lying! All you got to do is try it.

DAUGHTER. What? Snuff? That stinky stuff!

DEE DEE. Ain't you got no sense at all? Don't you know nothing?

DAUGHTER. How come you know so much?

DEE DEE. Oh, I forgot you ain't been to the river yet. There's a lot of things you don't know.

DAUGHTER. Have you ever tried it?

DEE DEE. What you think?

DAUGHTER. What it taste like?

DEE DEE. With milk it taste just like a chocolate milk shake. What you do is mix three big spoons of monkey dust in a glass of milk and drink it through a straw, fast. If you drink it all you'll wake up and be real pretty. Like them African dancing girls we saw on TV. They drink it everyday. It'll make your teeth white too. It's a secret though, and you got to swear on the Bible not to tell nobody.

DAUGHTER. All right.

DEE DEE. Go get Big Mama's Bible.

DAUGHTER. Girl, you crazy!

DEE DEE. You want to be pretty, don't you?

DAUGHTER. Yeah. *(Steps back, whispering to DEE DEE.)* She gonna beat my butt! *(Tiptoes towards BIG MAMA who is sleeping in her chair.)*

DEE DEE *(whispering back)*. Tell her you need it for Sunday School!

DAUGHTER *(reluctantly)*. All right.

DEE DEE. Repeat after me. I promise...*(DAUGHTER slips Bible away from BIG MAMA's lap. She dashes back to DEE DEE.)*

DAUGHTER. I promise...

Act I SHAKIN' THE MESS OUTTA MISERY Page 13

DEE DEE. ...not to tell nobody...Not Aunt Mae...Not Big Mama...Not Miss Mary...'Cause if I do...I'll turn into a monkey...You gonna be real pretty.

(Drinking from DEE DEE's cup, DAUGHTER gags. DEE DEE hides behind furniture as BIG MAMA wakes.)

BIG MAMA. What's the matter, baby? You get choked on something?

DAUGHTER. I fine, Big Mama.

BIG MAMA. What's all this? Child, what is going on here?

DAUGHTER. I ain't suppose to tell. I promised on the Bible. Big Mama, I don't want to go to hell.

BIG MAMA *(seizes Bible).* Uh huh! You gonna get me a switch off that bush if you don't tell me what's going on. You ain't going to hell for promising to keep something to yourself that ain't right.

DAUGHTER. Dee Dee said snuff was monkey dust and it make you real pretty.

BIG MAMA. Pretty is as pretty does. It's pretty ways that will get you in heaven. All the monkey dust in the world can't give you a good, kind, honest heart. I'm gonna switch the spite out of that Dee Dee.

DAUGHTER. Big Mama, why you dip snuff? That stuff is nasty.

BIG MAMA. Snuff ain't no worse than them cancer sticks that be killing folks left and right. Ain't never heard tell of snuff harming nobody. 'Cept the one time I recollect. Corine come close as green to a dollar to getting us killed on account of some snuff.

DAUGHTER. What happened, Big Mama?

BIG MAMA. Hold on, chile, I'm getting to it. A story ain't something you just read off like ingredients on a soap box.

A story's like a map, you follow the lines and they'll take you somewhere. There's a way to do anything and with a story you take your time. If you wanna hear, you got to listen.

DAUGHTER. I'm sorry. I'm listening, Big Mama.

BIG MAMA. Now, getting back to the story. It was a time when the only place colored folks could sit on a bus was in the back. But the number 99 was known as the Maid's Bus. It arrived downtown every weekday morning at 6 a.m. to pick up the colored domestic workers bound for the rich, white suburbs ninety minutes away. Now on this day, not only was the weather hot, but colored folks was stirred up over the lynching and the killings of colored peoples all over the south. A colored woman had just been found dead. She was raped and sawed open by six white men who made her brother watch 'em ravish her. The whites were getting meaner as the summer got hotter.

(YOUNG WOMAN, MISS MARY, and MISS CORINE march in singing a spirited gospel tune—they stand to wait for bus, fanning in the heat.)

MISS MARY. Ain't it hot.

MISS CORINE. Too hot to sit in the shade.

MISS MARY. Clothes dried stiff on the line before I finished the breakfast dishes yestiddy.

BIG MAMA. Some awful bloody things happened that summer.

MISS CORINE. It's 5:59 and there come Ralph, right on the dot.

(MISS LAMAMA rushes in.)

Act I   SHAKIN' THE MESS OUTTA MISERY   Page 15

MISS CORINE. Jessie Pearl, if you have anything to do with it you gonna be late for your own funeral.

MISS LAMAMA. Corine, you know I got to get my grandbabies to school on Friday.

MISS CORINE. I just know you be late all the time.

MISS LAMAMA. Did y'all hear? The young'uns is talking 'bout sittin' in at Woolworth's and boycottin' the busses.

MISS CORINE. I feel kinda proud about what they're doin'.

MISS MARY. Well, we won't have to worry about nothin', 'cause Doctor J.R. Whittenhauser done bought this number 99.

BIG MAMA. Yes ma'am, even if they was rioting downtown, white ladies in Northend were gonna have they meals cooked, babies looked after and laundry done. That's why they bought the bus. That morning I made the mistake of sittin' in Corine's seat. Now, conversations on the number 99 went something like this...

MISS CORINE. Now, shug, you gonna *have* to move. I been riding this bus for thirteen years and I ain't never sit nowhere else, but right here. It's plenty room in the back. This *my* seat and you just gonna *have* to move. *(Other WOMEN laugh.)* Well, y'all know this my seat. I always sit here. Oh Lord, my white lady asked me to come in on Sunday afternoon, would you believe, to pour tea for some English foreigners visiting her mama. I told her that her mama was gonna have to pour that tea herself, 'cause I had to go to church on Sunday. The Lord wouldn't appreciate my missing a prayer service to pour tea for the Queen of England.

MISS MARY. My white lady, bless her heart, is as simple as a chile. When the boss man was near 'bout fifty years old, he turn around and left the missus and two grown children to marry this girl right out of college. I knowed it was gonna happen, I seen it in a dream. This chile he married, believe me when I tell you, sends her drawers to the cleaners. Ain't that nothing? A grown woman that can't wash her own drawers.

MISS LAMAMA. Well the rest of us is maids on the job and off, but, Corine, you a professional. You got your training and everything and you ain't shamed to wear your uniform.

BIG MAMA. Nope, Corine wear her uniform just like a policeman. And she ain't no maid. She got them white folks calling her...

MISS CORINE. A Domestic Engineer. And my white people pay the price for having a professional in they service. Now Mary, you ought to be chargin' for your services too, 'cause you the one told me I was gonna hit the numbers last week, and told me some other things that come to pass. But now can you tell me where my spit cup is right now?

MISS MARY. Corine, I been telling you this as long as I knowed you and I done knowed you a mighty long time, it'd be highway robbery for me to charge money for a gift give to me by God.

BIG MAMA. Now, we was still in Northend where most of the rich white folk lived, when I took notice of this white Cadillac convertible cruising 'longside the bus. A red-faced white man was driving. A young white woman was sitting up there next to him with her long blond hair just blowing all around her face. Corine...you know Corine got to have her a dip of snuff don't care where she is or who she with, she gonna have herself a taste. This day wasn't no different, except that this day Corine didn't have her spit cup with her. She probably left it at her white lady's house.

MISS CORINE. Lamama, let me use your handkerchief.

MISS LAMAMA. Woman, you lost your mind? This my Ethiopian handkerchief.

Act I   SHAKIN' THE MESS OUTTA MISERY   Page 17

MISS CORINE. This a emergency...

MISS LAMAMA. No Lord, not this one.

MISS MARY. Use your bag.

MISS CORINE. I can't use my bag. I got them white folks lace table cloths in here. Shit, y'all, I got to spit somewhere. *(She spits out the window.)*

MISS MARY. Oooh, Corine! You done spit in that white woman's face! *(WOMEN all stare out of window.)*

BIG MAMA. Then we heard a siren and a policeman pulled the bus over. He talked to the white man some, then he got on the bus. Then he say: "Which one of you aunties spit in the lady's face? If don't nobody speak up right now, I'm gonna have to lock every one of you up. All right, I want all you niggers off the bus. That mean everybody. Line up over there." Cars was passing 'long the highway, with folks looking at us like we was from the moon. The white woman was leaning on the Cadillac looking mean and evil as a snake. I thought for sure we was gonna be killed. Then that white man stomp over to where we was lined up against the fence like dogs and hark spit on each one of us. Now Mary was behind me calling on her West Indian spirits and making signs. The white man laughed then he got into his Cadillac with his woman and pulled onto the highway. He drove right into the path of a tractor trailer truck. *(Each WOMAN wipes her own face, except for MISS LAMAMA, who wipes MISS CORINE's face with her Ethiopian handkerchief.)*

MISS MARY. You know the Lord works in mysterious ways.

MISS CORINE. And he sure don't like ugly.

BIG MAMA. I'll never forget it as long as I live. It was a mess of twisted white Cadillac, smoke and burning white flesh. Just a mess. Don't you never forget where we been, or that we got a long way to go.

DAUGHTER. Yes ma'am.

SCENE THREE

(Upbeat blues music.)

DAUGHTER. Wasn't long after Big Mama told me the story about the Maid's Bus that she come home with a woman I ain't never seen before. She was walking behind Big Mama, carrying a grocery sack. She walk real slow and sexy, look like she was smelling roses and time wasn't in her way. *(BIG MAMA has picked up her pocketbook and walks around the stage as if strolling around town. Walking back to DAUGHTER followed by MAGGIE carrying a grocery sack, they are moving in time with the music.)*

MAGGIE. Can I go now, lady?

BIG MAMA. Sit down.

MAGGIE. I got things to do.

BIG MAMA. You ain't going nowhere. You staying for dinner.

DAUGHTER. Who's that, Big Mama? What's her name?

BIG MAMA. Ask her yourself. She dumb but she ain't deaf.

MAGGIE. My name is Maggie Agatha Christmas St. Clair and I graduated high school and had some college so I ain't dumb.

BIG MAMA. I ain't said nothing 'bout no book learning. You ain't got no common sense and no conscience either. Down there on Kin Folks Corner trying to beat a old woman outta her money. You ought to be 'shamed of yourself. They teach you that in college?

MAGGIE. I was tired of making a living on my back.

Act I SHAKIN' THE MESS OUTTA MISERY Page 19

DAUGHTER. On your back?

MAGGIE. Ain't nobody ever wanted me for Maggie. They either wanted something from me or they took it without asking. At least now I'm making a living for myself.

BIG MAMA. That ain't no livin'. Jail's full of girls think like that. Ain't no reason for you not to use your Godgiven potential. Daughter, show Maggie where she can wash up. *(DAUGHTER and MAGGIE go to vanity.)* Dinner be ready directly. *(Pause.)* We poor, but I know each piece of jewelry I got, so wash the honey off your hands.

DAUGHTER. You got pretty hair.

MAGGIE. Thank you, 'lil sister. You got pretty eyes.

DAUGHTER. Thank you.

MAGGIE. Can you wink your eyes?

DAUGHTER. No.

MAGGIE. I'm gonna teach you how to wink, 'lil sister. With eyes pretty as yours it'll come in handy.

DAUGHTER. You gonna stay with us now?

MAGGIE. Depends, 'lil sister, on the way the wind blow in the morning.

DAUGHTER. You really do that with men for money?

MAGGIE. I made some mistakes I hope you never have to.

DAUGHTER. Maggie, was you ever in love?

MAGGIE. I been in love too many times to count. If love was a dollar bill, I'd be a millionaire. And if pain was a quarter, it would be triple. *(Extends her hand.)* Do you know what this is?

DAUGHTER. Your hand?

MAGGIE. Look at this, that's my love line. It's broken. And it ain't very long. That should've been my first sign. You want to hear about the first man I fell in love with?

DAUGHTER. Yes ma'am!

MAGGIE. I knowed he was whorish. When I met him he was married and tipping out on his wife. I never figured he'd tip out on me. That was my downfall. His name was Johnny Earl Davis. He would come to the Dew Drop Inn where I was singing and make love to me with his eyes. Chills run up and down my spine when I catch his eyes all over me like that. Pretty soon he was all I could see... smell...taste...or touch. When he asked me to marry him, we almost broke that hotel bed celebrating the engagement. Our love-making was like two freight trains meeting head-on—Chile, he was my thunder and honey. A week before my wedding I went shopping for my wedding dress. I bought myself a real expensive white wool suit with pearl buttons and white gloves, shoes, pocketbook and hat to match. I had to admit I looked good—sharp as a tack. I even bought a little see-through nightgown for the wedding night and got some love oil from the hoodoo woman to keep his nature up all night. I was ready. Then, the day of my wedding Johnny Earl Davis call my mama's house and said he had another woman. Say he still loved me but she must have worked a root on him 'cause he just can't help hisself. It like to cut me to the bone. I got in my car and went from joint to joint looking for him. When I found him, he was all dressed up, getting out of a brand new car. I tried to run him down like the dog he was. I heard a few months after I broke his leg and run over his foot, that the woman he was with took all his money and left him. And you know something, 'lil sister, I hope that son-of-a... cockroach is still sucking rocks. One good thing came out of it and that was a song. Say, "The Blues Ain't Nuthin' But a Good Woman Feeling Bad." You got to live the blues to sing them, 'lil sister. *(Puts her wig on DAUGH-TER's head.)*

Act I   SHAKIN' THE MESS OUTTA MISERY   Page 21

DAUGHTER. You can be my mama if you want to.

MAGGIE. Where your mama?

DAUGHTER. She up north. It's been a long time since I seen her. She's a dancer. If she was here she'd show me how to dance.

MAGGIE. I'm gonna show you, 'lil sister. Gonna show you how to dance. *(Upbeat blues from top of scene. MAGGIE teaches DAUGHTER dance steps.)* Come on now. Just follow me. That's it. Now put a little something in it. Shake your moneymaker. Yeah, you got it, girl.

DAUGHTER. See, Mama, I can dance! Maggie stayed with us all summer, dancing, cooking, telling stories. Every new moon she used to scrub down the house with hot soapy water mixed with a few drops of holy water she stole from the Catholic church. She was using the holy water to protect the house from evil. One time I asked her why she needed protection. "Don't God hear you when you pray?"

MAGGIE. Yeah, baby, he hears me, but even God needs a back-up.

DAUGHTER. I wasn't a believer at the time so I bust out laughing. But the time Aunt Mae got that growth in her stomach, made a believer out of me. Aunt Mae had a way of keeping Jesus in every conversation. She and Big Mama sure was blood sisters. Them women loved the Lord.

SCENE FOUR

SCENE: *BIG MAMA sits in her chair as AUNT MAE enters.*

AUNT MAE. Sister?

BIG MAMA. Good Lord, Mae! If I didn't know better I'd swear you was fixing to have twins. What the doctor say?

AUNT MAE. What them fools know about God's creation? They talking about operating on me!

BIG MAMA. Sis, no!

AUNT MAE. I been with a uncut belly this long, I believe I'll just keep on till Jesus takes me home.

BIG MAMA. Don't talk like that, Mae Francis. Something got to be done.

AUNT MAE. I've been to see Doctor Willie.

BIG MAMA. That man ain't no doctor!

AUNT MAE. He's the best in the business.

BIG MAMA. Where he get his degree, the grocery store? Willie Green sell roots and tree branches...

AUNT MAE. What colored folk do before they send these young boys to doctor on us? You'd do well to see Doctor Willie about your high blood pressure.

BIG MAMA. I'm doing just fine, thank you, with my doctor, my medication and the good Lord's will. You'd do well to speak with Lamama about her husband, you so quick to fix things.

AUNT MAE. Otis is a paying customer.

BIG MAMA. It's still a sin, Mae Francis.

AUNT MAE. I give a service to the community. If Otis didn't give his money to me he'd find somebody else to sell it to him. He don't come but once a week.

BIG MAMA. On Sunday! It ain't right no way you look at it. Selling liquor on the Lord's day.

AUNT MAE. Anybody over fifty-one can sit in my kitchen, pay for a drink of uncut liquor and get a little companionship throwed in for free. It's like a social club. Besides, I'm a businesswoman, sister, I got to make a living like anybody else, you know that.

BIG MAMA. I know you do just what you please. Folks talking.

Act I SHAKIN' THE MESS OUTTA MISERY Page 23

AUNT MAE. They talked about Jesus Christ.

BIG MAMA. You ain't Jesus.

AUNT MAE. And you ain't Mary. Stop acting like you ain't never had a good time. I remember more times than one Daddy had to drag you out of many a juke joint.

BIG MAMA. Never said I was a saint. I've made some mistakes, but that still don't make what you doing right.

AUNT MAE. Don't make it wrong. *(Silence.)* Let's don't fuss, sister, I got too many other things on my mind.

BIG MAMA. We got to take care, sister. You and Daughter all I got. Let's don't fall out over nothing. Time's too short. *(BIG MAMA and AUNT MAE hug. BIG MAMA starts arranging chairs, DAUGHTER begins to pour tea.)*

DAUGHTER. Big Mama being Aunt Mae's closest living kin, called a special meeting of the number 2 Mission Prayer Circle to pray over her. Come dark and just shadows apart, three elder sisters of the church eased in the back door. Miss Mary, Miss Corine, with her spit cup, and Miss Rosa. Miss Rosa was kinda different from other folks, from being around so many dead people. She ran the funeral home down on Front Street. And late as always came Miss Lamama.

(The WOMEN enter one at a time. They talk, take tea and a seat, making a half-circle.)

MISS LAMAMA. Lord, I had quite a walk here, ladies.

MISS CORINE. Ain't but two block, Lamama. I know you not that old.

MISS LAMAMA. Ain't but two blocks, but I had to stop and talk to Sister Alice. You do know Sister Davis died?

BIG MAMA. Have mercy.

MISS LAMAMA. There's going to be a fight, I can just feel it. Those children of hers will be Rosa's next customers, 'cause they are gonna kill each other over that insurance money.

MISS MARY. Speaking of killing, look here, Lamama, I've been meaning to ask you, is that husband of your sister's still giving her trouble?

MISS LAMAMA. Monday week I come home from church and on my word, sisters, my mama's antique upright piano was missing. Come to find out Henry done pawned it to pay off his gambling debts. Lord, what she gonna do?

BIG MAMA. Have faith and keep praying over it. The Lord will make a way...in the meantime, seem to me like she better put a lock on the kitchen sink.

MISS CORINE. Or a knock upside his head, now that'll fix him.

AUNT MAE *(calmly stirring her tea)*. A man is only good for a few things and if he can't do them right you don't need him. You can do poorly by yourself. *(Several amens are heard.)*

MISS LAMAMA. If you can keep him at home.

AUNT MAE. That's up to him.

MISS LAMAMA. If he was left alone maybe he could find his way home.

AUNT MAE. All the men I know got a mind of they own and know where they want to be and with who.

MISS LAMAMA *(stands up)*. Outside of shut up, I just wanna say one thing to you, Mae Francis...

MISS CORINE. It's getting hot in here.

MISS LAMAMA. Leave my husband alone.

MISS CORINE. Otis ain't worth it.

MISS MARY. Ain't no man worth it.

AUNT MAE. You put a lock on him, it ain't my place.

Act I   SHAKIN' THE MESS OUTTA MISERY   Page 25

MISS LAMAMA. Don't you talk to me that way.

BIG MAMA. Ladies! Now I want to call this meeting of the number 2 Mission Prayer Circle to order. *(Notices DAUGHTER.)* Chile, what you still doing down here? Go on upstairs so us grown folks can meet.

DAUGHTER. Can I stay for...*(BIG MAMA gives her a look. WOMEN take their places.)*

BIG MAMA. Is there any old business we need to take care of? All right then, Sister Lamama's gonna read her report on the activities of the missionary to the sick.

MISS LAMAMA. Thank you. On Thursday, August the 15th, Sister Mary Joseph and myself called on three sick members of the congregation of the Eight Street Baptist Church. Now I've already reported that Sister Davis died, God rest her soul. Sister English is recuperating at St. Mother Mary's Hospital in satisfactory condition from her gall bladder operation. She says she appreciates the chewing tobacco and peppermint candies that we took up collection to buy for her. Now Brother Solomon's cataract operation was a success. He says it's scandalous though, how short them nurses are wearing they uniforms. He's seeing more now than he ever wanted to. Brother Solomon's sister told me...

BIG MAMA *(interrupting)*. Thank you for your report, Jessie Pearl. I believe Sister Mary wanna begin her reading of the scripture. *(MISS MARY stands to read with much feeling, a rising fervor. Her last lines are spoken as if she is about to shout. The WOMEN saying amens, etc., all the while.)*

AUNT MAE. Thank you.

MISS MARY. Now, I'll be reading today from the fifth chapter of James, verses 13 through 15. "Is any among you afflicted?"

AUNT MAE. Yes Lord.

MISS MARY. "Let him pray. Is any merry? Let him sing psalms. Is any sick among you? Let him call for the elders of the church and let them pray over him, anointing him with oil in the name of the Lord. And the prayer of faith shall save the sick and the Lord shall raise him up; And if he have committed sins, they shall be forgiven him." The almighty Jesus said: "Daughter, be of good comfort, thy faith has made thee whole." Hallelujiah! *(BIG MAMA has begun singing an uplifting spiritual. The WOMEN are clapping, MISS CORINE jumps to her feet, eyes closed, does a little dance, shakes her tambourine. The other WOMEN join in. AUNT MAE jumps to her feet and begins to testify as the WOMEN continue to sing, hum and moan.)*

AUNT MAE. I wanna testify, sistren. In this, the prime part of my life, I been afflicted with a tumor and a doctor, both have given me nothing but misery. They wants to operate on this body of mine that's weak from carrying loads Jesus saw fit for me to carry. For these many years the Lord has made a way. I'm gonna keep on believing in brighter days ahead. I just ask that this load of mine be lightened so I can continue to do God's work. In the Lord's name I pray. Blessed be to the Holy Ghost. Amen. Yes, Lord, Yes, Jesus. *(DAUGHTER, who has been caught up in the mood, jumps up.)*

DAUGHTER. Yes, Jesus! *(The WOMEN stop and stare a moment.)*

BIG MAMA *(seats AUNT MAE as she speaks)*. Sister, we all gathered here this evening 'cause there is a sister among us needing a healing. My sister Mae Francis has had a report from the doctor that says she needs a operation, but all of us know from experience that the Lord can provide us with miracle. Sisters, let us pray.

DAUGHTER. The sisters of the number 2 Mission Prayer Circle kept coming to our living room every Tuesday night to testify, sing, preach and pray over Aunt Mae. In the middle of one meeting Aunt Mae fell out. I knew she was dead. But Big Mama laid hands on her and it brought her back to life. Big Mama be dealing serious. Looking at Big Mama nobody could tell just how much power she had over people and folks was constantly giving credit to God. Eight weeks to the day after the first prayer meeting was called Aunt Mae reported that her tumor had disappeared.

AUNT MAE. It was the prayers of the faithful and the will of God made me well. Amen.

ALL WOMEN. Hallelujiah!

DAUGHTER. But me, I knew it was Big Mama again, shaking the mess outta misery. *(WOMEN exit singing the uplifting spiritual.)*

END ACT ONE

ACT TWO

SCENE: *DAUGHTER on stage. MISS LAMAMA enters and mimes hanging clothes on the line.*

DAUGHTER. As time got closer for me to go the the river, I started spending more time alone with my Big Mamas, women who gave stories as gifts. Miss Lamama was special in that. Being married to an African, Miss Lamama learned their tradition of storytelling. She wore pink slippers everyday but Sunday when she sang in the choir. I loved hearing her catch notes with her voice and then letting them fly over our heads into the congregation like birds. When Miss Lamama was telling a story her voice was like that too.

MISS LAMAMA. Now, Daughter, I'm gonna tell you about the time Miss Shine got even for a four hundred-year-old wrong, as it was told to me. And 'long as I'm black I'll never forget it.

(MISS SHINE enters and mimes rolling in tea cart.)

MISS LAMAMA. Miss Shine lived down the street from us. She had worked in the governor's mansion ever since her husband had died and left her with no insurance and a lot of bills to pay. But Miss Shine caught on quick that the governor and his wife was just simple country crackers. The funniest thing she had to do was pour tea everyday at four o'clock for the governor and his wife. They would sit there in the living room, quiet as two rocks in a river, slurping that sweet tea till suppertime. This particular December, our colored high school chorus was selected to sing at the governor's mansion on Christmas Eve. For weeks that's all folk talked about.

MISS SHINE. You know I'm gonna be there to see our children show out. The governor done asked me already to stay past sundown on Christmas Eve.

MISS LAMAMA. Weeks before the first Christmas pine was chopped, Miss Shine was busy polishing cabinets full of silver and starching closets full of linen. Her biggest job, and one she loved best and saved for last, was cleaning the grand French crystal chandelier that hung in the entry hall to the mansion.

MISS SHINE. It gimme time to think.

MISS LAMAMA. Two days before the singing a strong feeling came over Miss Shine like something bad was about to happen. But, Christmas Eve when she seen them three yellow school buses roll around the circle driveway, Miss Shine's heart was near 'bout busting with joy. She knowed we were gonna do her proud that night. Them little white children was dressed up in blue jackets for the boys and blue skirts for the girls. But we had on long white robes with gold sashes over our shoulders looking just like black angels. The first group of them little white children sang they Christmas carols in high pitched cut-off notes that didn't sound right to Miss Shine, but she clapped when they was done. The second group wasn't much better, but, Lord, then them colored children broke loose. I led the choir. When we was done there was a deep hush, quiet like even God had stopped what *she* was doing to listen. Then they sent for the children to come inside for hot chocolate.

But that governor only invited them white children inside for hot chocolate. Our faces went soft and sad like they was gonna cry. Except for Corine. Her face was hard like she wanted to throw a brick through that mansion window. Your Big Mama looked like she didn't 'spect no less. Shine looked at us, something inside of her broke in two.

MISS SHINE. She was madder than a foam-mouth dog. But what could she do? She left it in the Lord's hands, and he came through. With no warning, the big, round crystal that hung from the middle of the chandelier fell with a loud crash on the marble floor, breaking into a million pieces. It didn't hurt nobody, but Shine took it to be a sign.

MISS LAMAMA. Miss Emmie seen Shine staring and snapped up "Shine, get a broom and sweep up this mess before one of the children gets hurt."

MISS SHINE. She swept up every piece of crystal she could find. They sparkled like diamonds, but every jagged edge was a dagger in her heart. Folks say things changed, but it's still like slavery times, Miss Shine's mind eased back, way, way back. She heard a chant far off and deep as slave graves and old Africa.

MISS LAMAMA *(beats her calabash in time)*. Blood, boil thick, run red like a river, slave scream, wail, moan after they dead. Daddy lynched, Mama raped, baby sister sold down river. Slaves scream, wail, moan after they dead. The cook knew what to do to save the race, stop the screams.

MISS SHINE. Miss Shine all of a sudden knowed what she had to do to save the race. She was possessed by her power. When she got home she went into her bedroom and she got the wood bowl her mama give her and the iron head of her husband's hammer. She come back to the table spread with all the broke crystal and ground it till sweat dripped off her face into the bowl. And she ground it, and she ground it and she ground it till it was fine as dust. Then she tied it in a corner of her slip. When Miss Shine has to go back to work after New Year's she was ready, almost happy to go.

MISS LAMAMA. Miss Emmie stopped her from washing the lunch dishes to tell her, "Shine, we ready for tea." Miss Shine yes ma'amed her, looking direct in her eyes. Miss Emmie wasn't used to colored making eye contact and she near 'bout run out the kitchen. Miss Shine went on as usual fixing tea. She put the kettle on to boil.

DAUGHTER and MISS LAMAMA. Blood boil thick.

MISS LAMAMA. She kept hearing whispers. She poured the boiling water over the tea leaves and strained it into the big silver teapot.

DAUGHTER and MISS LAMAMA. Run red like a raging river.

MISS LAMAMA. She took down two china cups with a flower pattern and set 'em straight on matching saucers.

DAUGHTER and MISS LAMAMA. Nobody know how the master get sick.

MISS LAMAMA. Miss Shine put everything on the big tea cart.

DAUGHTER and MISS LAMAMA. Nobody know how he die.

MISS LAMAMA. She untied the knot in the corner of her slip and emptied the fine crystals into the sugar bowl and...

DAUGHTER and MISS LAMAMA. Stirred it up, stirred it up, stirred it up goooood. *(Sighs of relief.)*

MISS LAMAMA. Miss Shine kept pouring tea for the governor and Miss Emmie for more than two weeks before she disappeared. Some folks say she moved to an entirely colored town in Texas, other folks say she wasn't really of this world in the first place. Nobody ever see Miss Shine again. From then on, the colored high school chorus started singing Christmas carols at the colored nursing home every year to honor our own folks. Nobody ever talk about wanting to sing for the governor no more. Every time I sing "Spirit of the Living God" solo, I dedicate it to Miss Shine, wherever she is. Daughter, remember, you must always honor your ancestors.

DAUGHTER. Yes ma'am. There are all kinds of gifts you can give and receive, Miss Lamama's was pride. *(MISS LAMAMA exits singing line from mournful gospel.)*

SCENE TWO

SCENE: *AUNT MAE enters straightening up room.*

DAUGHTER. Miss Lamama's second husband, Mr. Otis, kept Aunt Mae company on Sunday afternoons in her upstairs bedroom. He drove a taxi cab everyday 'cept Sunday, when he would show up at Aunt Mae's and give me a dime to go catch the ice cream truck, making me promise to play on the porch till the street lights came on. That's when he would go home to Miss Lamama. Every Sunday Aunt Mae and Mr. Otis kept the door closed and the gospel singing on the radio turned up loud. Once I asked her, "What ya'll be doing in the room with the door closed?"

AUNT MAE. We be taking care of grown folks business.

DAUGHTER. One Sunday, Miss Lamama come knocking on the front door.

MISS LAMAMA. Tell your Aunt Mae Miss Lamama wanna talk to her.

Act II   SHAKIN' THE MESS OUTTA MISERY

DAUGHTER. Yes ma'am. Aunt Mae! *(DAUGHTER runs to the bedroom door, scared, and whispers.)* Aunt Mae! Miss Lamama at the door. She wanna talk to you.

AUNT MAE. Tell her I be right there.

DAUGHTER. She coming, Miss Lamama. *(DAUGHTER goes to hide behind furniture. AUNT MAE strolls out of the bedroom slowly.)*

AUNT MAE. What you want, Jessie Pearl?

MISS LAMAMA. Want you to know you can have him.

AUNT MAE *(looks at MISS LAMAMA stunned, then laughs her rowdy laugh).* Have him?

MISS LAMAMA. I mean it, Mae Francis. Since Otis took up with you, all I had is trouble. Folks talk. Even the pastor know where Otis be on Sunday after church. I'm through. *(She slaps her hands together and turns away.)*

AUNT MAE. You got the wrong idea, Jessie Pearl. I don't need a husband. I ain't got time to take care of one. What I have is a liquor business.

MISS LAMAMA. Otis ain't bought groceries for over two years. Told me his mama in Ohio needed some operations. I found out she been dead ten years. Tell him his clothes be on the front porch this evening. G'night, Mae Francis, see you in choir rehearsal. *(MISS LAMAMA exits slowly, proudly. AUNT MAE is angry.)*

AUNT MAE. Men like that give me a bad name. I try to give married women a break. I don't want to be cause of no major interference like that.

DAUGHTER. Aunt Mae went back upstairs and a few seconds later, Mr. Otis come running out the front door tryin' to catch up with Miss Lamama.

AUNT MAE *(re-enters bedroom and speaks to Otis).* Get out of my house now, you no good lyin' skunk butt and don't come round here no more. That means till hell freeze over.

DAUGHTER. Me and Aunt Mae ran to the living room window, both of us laughing out loud at the sight of Mr. Otis running on drunk legs behind Miss Lamama with his shirttails flying in the wind.

AUNT MAE. Women got to stick together. Now, Daughter, get your cup. *(AUNT MAE pours them both a drink.)* Daughter, please promise me something.

DAUGHTER. What, Aunt Mae?

AUNT MAE. Don't you ever, long as grass is green, go nowhere with a man unless you got some money in your pocket. If you with a man that don't mean you no good, you can always tell him to go to the devil and catch you a taxi cab or a Greyhound bus home. Promise me, baby, will you?

DAUGHTER. Yes ma'am. I promise. Aunt Mae and Miss Lamama were almost friends after that. Aunt Mae didn't seem to miss Mr. Otis none. The things I learned about love. All kinds of possibilities. *(Upbeat blues intro for next scene.)*

SCENE THREE

DAUGHTER. When the Sunday-after-dark crowd came later that night, Aunt Mae was laughing loud and cussing like it was any other Sunday. Most Sunday evenings after the sun settled down and darkness fell round Aunt Mae's house, she could be found sitting like a queen at the head of her kitchen table pouring short glasses of whiskey for women Big Mama said was loose and men she said was loud. I usually sat on a stool by the refrigerator drinking ginger ale and two splashes in a Dixie cup pretending to be just one of the crowd.

(MISS TOM and MISS CORINE enter.)

DAUGHTER. Hey, Miss Tom. Hey, Miss Corine. *(WOMEN greet DAUGHTER and AUNT MAE. Each woman throws a coin into a glass bowl and picks up the drink AUNT MAE pours for her.)* Oh, Miss Tom, Billy and Ray Lee got in a fight. I saw 'em out my window last night.

MISS TOM. What you doing up that late?

AUNT MAE. Hey, Tom, where your sister at tonight?

MISS TOM. Lily at the clinic patching up some more Negroes done cut each other up last night.

MISS CORINE *(playfully)*. Mae Francis, you know Lily and Tom ain't no sisters. More like man and wife, ain't it, Tom?

MISS TOM. You keep talking and you gonna need patching up. Now get out of my business and take care of your own. If I say she my sister, she my sister. Ain't got to be by blood.

AUNT MAE. Amen. Awoman. Hey, Corine, what you be doing round Kin Folks Corner late at night?

MISS CORINE. Who told you that? I've been working with Doctor Willie as an apprentice.

MISS TOM. You call picking roots and berries, quacking and running numbers work?

MISS CORINE. Doctor Willie didn't pick up root work off the corner, it's a science. Doctor Willie apprenticed with a one hundred percent pure Cherokee Injun medicine man.

AUNT MAE. I got Injun blood in me too.

MISS TOM. What Negro don't?

MISS CORINE. My great-grandma was pure dee Injun. She live to be 105 years old. She the one took me back to the reservation to meet the medicine man. He taught me some things that can't be found in the history books. The Injuns was doing just fine before the white man come here, living on land that didn't belong to nobody, taking care of business.

DAUGHTER *(trying to get her attention).* Aunt Mae. Aunt Mae. Tell me about the time you was a dance hall girl.

MISS TOM. Lord, Jesus, I don't want to hear that one!

AUNT MAE *(laughs wickedly).* Ain't you heard them old tales enough to tell 'em to me?

DAUGHTER. I wanna hear. You tell 'em better. Tell me 'bout the fat men. Please, Aunt Mae, please. *(MISS TOM dances with AUNT MAE, mimes fat man, encourages AUNT MAE. Upbeat blues from opening.)*

AUNT MAE. I used to waltz, jitterbug or whatever was called for around the dance floor with customers for a dime a dance. Fat men were the worst. Yes ma'am, they was a curse to us working girls. All they ever wanna do is hug up and grind. So I used to plump myself up with a pillow to keep 'em from getting too close to my privates. Now some of them mens said they wanted to take care of me. They was expecting a compromise on my part that I could not make. I was too independent to take like that without giving. I always have been my own woman. Take marriage, for instance. Now that's a job, darling, and I earned my way dollar for dollar. I put up with other women, drinking and gambling but the one thing I would not tolerate was a liar. I threw Mason Pew out of his own house two days after I married him for lying to me.

DAUGHTER. Did you let him come back, Aunt Mae?

AUNT MAE. No ma'am.

MISS CORINE. Tell the truth now.

Act II SHAKIN' THE MESS OUTTA MISERY Page 37

AUNT MAE. I'm telling the story. He wasn't too proud to beg. I told him to get up off his rusty knees and out of my face. I didn't want to hear that mess. Wasn't no room in my life for liars, that's all there was to it.

DAUGHTER. What you do when he left?

AUNT MAE. You mean when I put him out. Honey, it was like the Fourth of July, when the smoke cleared I felt free.

DAUGHTER. So why you get married in the first place?

AUNT MAE. Why anybody would, for security. And on top of that, Mason Pew was good looking.

MISS CORINE. He was good looking.

AUNT MAE. Lord knows that was a good looking man. But his lying took something out of me. I took him back in my house, but I never took him back in my heart. Don't let nobody fool you, sex is something you can live without for a long time. Like my mama told me, if it gets hot, fan it. Love only last till the shine wear off. *(The WOMEN toast to that last line.)*

DAUGHTER. When people used to ask me what I wanted to be when I grew up, I'd say, "I wanna be like Aunt Mae. I wanna be independent so every day be like the Fourth of July."

ALL WOMEN. Amen, chile. *(WOMEN exit. DAUGHTER and MISS TOM walk off to fishing area.)*

SCENE FOUR

SCENE: *DAUGHTER and MISS TOM sit on stage, apparently fishing.*

DAUGHTER. Me and Miss Tom were friends, good friends. She taught me how to fish, throw a knife, carve a piece of wood, tame birds and believe in a world of impossibilities. Miss Tom was not a pretty woman, she was handsome like a man. Her hands were big, thick and callused. But she had a woman's eyes, dark and mysterious eyes, that held woman secrets, eyes that had seen miracles and reflected love like only a woman can.

MISS TOM. Let me tell you something, baby. It's people that keep bad luck in your house. That's why I try to keep 'em out of my house and out of my business.

DAUGHTER. What we got to catch with today?

MISS TOM. We got a sardine, some Vienna sausages and canned corn. These old crafty swimmers do like that canned corn. But the fish kinda slow this morning.

DAUGHTER. They slow every time we come here. I don't know why we can't go to the lake? It's a lot of people over there.

MISS TOM. You seen any colored people over there?

DAUGHTER. No ma'am.

MISS TOM. Enough said.

DAUGHTER. Why people different? How come we ain't all the same?

MISS TOM. Wouldn't be as interesting everybody be the same. Be like eating peas and potatoes everyday of your life.

DAUGHTER. I eat grits every day.

MISS TOM. Ain't very interesting, is it?

DAUGHTER. No ma'am. *(Silence.)* Miss Tom, you the only lady carpenter I know of. Could I be a lady carpenter when I grow up?

MISS TOM. Peaches, you can be anything you want.

DAUGHTER. Could I marry a woman and live with her like you do with Miss Lily?

Act II SHAKIN' THE MESS OUTTA MISERY Page 39

MISS TOM. Let me put it to you like this, there's all kind of possibilities for love. I didn't have no choice 'bout who to love, my heart just reached out and grabbed ahold of Miss Lily. She felt the same way I felt, so we lived together. Been together twenty-two years this May. You still got a lot of time to figure out that part of living.

DAUGHTER. How will I know if I'm in love?

MISS TOM. You won't have to ask nobody, you'll know.

DAUGHTER. Was my mama in love?

MISS TOM. I 'spect she must've been. You figure. This slick-talking beauty supply salesman driving a yellow convertible come to call on Corine's shop where Fannie Mae was fixing hair. He offered her a piece of the road, she dropped that greasy hot comb she was holding and they lit out of town in a cloud of fine red dust. You could say she had some kind of feeling.

DAUGHTER. Why couldn't I go with her?

MISS TOM. Your mama didn't just up and leave you out of spite for wanting the high life. She left here intending to make a better life for you and her. Your mama had the courage to reach. Colored folks, as you know, are the most amazing people on this earth. Anything we put our minds to and our hearts into we can get done good, and most times better than that. You'll never know if you can do a thing till you try. And a try has never failed.

DAUGHTER. Yes ma'am. *(Mimes catching fish.)* Oh!

MISS TOM. Hey, look like we gonna have fish for dinner after all.

DAUGHTER. That morning clicked the lock in our friendship, but that was the last time Miss Tom took me fishing. Like she predicted to Big Mama, my interest soon turned to other young folk. But I'll never forget Miss Tom. She and Miss Lily's spirits probably still live in that big, old, white house, loving each other with their eyes wide open.

SCENE FIVE

DAUGHTER. I remember the day that Dee Dee came running into my room all out of breath. "Fannie Mae's dead," she said. I almost asked her who she was talking about. All I could think of to say was: "I guess I don't get to go up north now." I used to hate Fannie Mae for being dead. Big Mama? What cause my mama to die?

(WOMEN enter in funeral clothes/hats softly singing African ritual song from opening. "Yemenjah ah say sool, ah say sool Yemenjah.")

BIG MAMA. Hard headed just like you.
DAUGHTER. Miss Mary, was my mother stubborn?
MISS MARY. Fannie Mae knew her mind and spoke it.
DAUGHTER. Why my mama have to be the one to die?
AUNT MAE. I loved her hard as I love you, but love ain't never saved nobody from dying. *(WOMEN begin to march into scene. Solemn gospel music.)*
DAUGHTER. The only way I can picture her now is asleep at her funeral. I remember sitting on the last pew in the church, all dressed up, with Aunt Mae on one side of me and Miss Corine on the other. The singing that day was sad and I could hear people up in the front hollering and crying. Then they led me up to the front of the church and held me up over the long, white casket surrounded by flowers. Fannie Mae was laying inside looking like she had

fallen asleep. She was so beautiful it made my throat hurt to look at her.

AUNT MAE. Do you know who that is?

DAUGHTER. It's Fannie Mae, ain't it?

AUNT MAE. She's in the Lord's hands now. We don't have to worry about her being too pretty no more. She through dancing now.

DAUGHTER. Big Mama say I leaned over that casket and kissed her, right on the lips. Miss Rosa prepared her for burial. She sure did make her look pretty. *(ALL WOMEN except MISS ROSA exit.)* Big Mama said Miss Rosa had habits that would drive Jesus to take a drink of whiskey. One Sunday I met up with Miss Rosa on my way to church.

MISS ROSA. Morning, Daughter.

DAUGHTER. Morning.

MISS ROSA. Pretty flowers you have on.

DAUGHTER. Thank you. Big Mama made me wear 'em.

MISS ROSA. Well now, what in the world is wrong with that? It's Mother's Day, isn't it? The red flower is for your living Big Mamas. And that there white flower's so your blood mama know you haven't forgotten her. You know you got to respect the dead as well as the living.

DAUGHTER. Miss Rosa, I do want to thank you for making my mama look so pretty at her funeral.

MISS ROSA. Fannie Mae's passing was a great loss to us all. Sometimes she was the most stubborn creature, wouldn't listen to nothing and nobody. Other times she was sweet as sugar. She was caught in a change. Look like you at that bend in the road now. Pay good attention to the road you travel.

DAUGHTER. Yes ma'am. Grown folks could be so mysterious about certain things. Big Mama and Aunt Mae would bend my ears back about obeying God and my elders. Talk about everybody and everything 'cept my blood mama Fannie Mae. One time I heard somebody say she died from dancin'. Somebody else I heard say she died from an old wound that was too deep to heal. But when I wanted someone to remember my mama to me, all the begging I could manage wouldn't move them to talk much about her.

SCENE SIX

DAUGHTER. The morning of the day I was going to the river, Big Mama sent me to Miss Corine's to get my hair done. I decided that if anybody was going to tell me about Fannie Mae, it was going to be Miss Corine. She knew everybody's business. Because she ran the beauty shop she was in a position to listen in on everybody's life, first, second and third hand. She was also in a position to give her opinion on a lot of things. Standing over somebody's head for two or more hours does gain their full attention. A crooked hand-lettered sign was stuck in the corner of her kitchen window announcing: "Miss Corine's Beauty Shop, We Curl Up And Dye." Once inside the back door of her kitchen, the strong scent of Sulphur Eight hair grease was like a salve to my soul. I knew I wasn't far from a good feeling. Good morning, Miss Corine.

MISS CORINE. Hey, chile. You ready for your trip to the river?

DAUGHTER. Yes ma'am.

MISS CORINE. C'mon, get up in the chair. Now I'm just gonna grease and plait it up 'cause we gotta wrap it up real special for the crossing over, okay? Lord have mercy, look

Act II   SHAKIN' THE MESS OUTTA MISERY   Page 43

at this kitchen. I'm gonna have to put the hot comb to this. Hold your ear.

DAUGHTER. Miss Corine, how long you know my blood mama?

MISS CORINE. Chile, I knowed your mama before she was knee-high to a duck. She worked here in my shop for two years.

DAUGHTER. Big Mama and Aunt Mae won't tell me much about her. They say it hurt too much. But I gotta know what happen to her. Please tell me, Miss Corine.

MISS CORINE. Your mama's pride was her long, pretty hair, a good grade and thick, too. Just like yours. Fannie Mae always had her nose stuck in a fashion magazine. If she said it once she said it a thousand times, "Miss Corine, I'm going to New York and wear dresses like that and when I do my dance everybody gonna scream."

(FANNIE MAE enters dancing.)

MISS CORINE. When she turned fifteen she got a scholarship to a little dance school downtown. One day Fannie Mae got to dancing through the park them white folks claimed was theirs. Some white boys run up behind her. Them boys raped her right there in that park in broad daylight. She fought back, though. When the police come, she carried on so they took her to the mental ward. When they got her in that hospital them animals shaved that poor chile's head clean. *(MISS CORINE wraps DAUGHTER's head in a white scarf.)* She bent after that. All your mama ever wanted was to dance. Her dream was to dance all over the world. The closest your mama come to her dream was cleaning up in a dance hall. Now that's all I know. It wasn't a pretty picture but it's the one I saw. If you don't remember nothing else your Big Mamas tell you, I want you to remember this, if you got a dance or dream or anything at all, don't let nothing or nobody get in your way. We ain't saying it's gonna be easy, but we all got a dance to do. You remember this, you hear?

(BIG MAMA enters.)

DAUGHTER. Thank you, Miss Corine. *(DAUGHTER, with head wrapped, goes to BIG MAMA.)* Miss Corine told me about the bad things that happened to my mama. But she didn't tell me how she died.

BIG MAMA. It was wrong of me not to tell you before now. I been praying for the strength to pass on this part to you. It was like this, Daughter, one morning she called me and told me she dreamed she grew wings. I knew that was a bad sign, so I went up to New York to try to get her to come home so we could heal her. She wouldn't leave New York. I could already see her slipping away. Just before daybreak she tried to fly. Jumped right out that window. I watched her break into thousand pieces. That's how we lost her. But we still got you and you got all of us. You ever been hungry? You ever need something these women didn't do without to give you? We love you, Daughter. Any woman can have a baby, but it takes a special woman to be a mama. You remember that, you hear?

DAUGHTER. Yes ma'am. *(They embrace and BIG MAMA leads DAUGHTER around the circle of WOMEN singing Yemenjah song.)*

MISS MARY. I love you, baby.

MISS LAMAMA. I love you, peaches.

AUNT MAE. I love you, Daughter.

MISS CORINE. I love you, little mama.

Act II SHAKIN' THE MESS OUTTA MISERY

MAGGIE. I love you, 'lil sister. *(WOMEN hum.)*

BIG MAMA. "Welcome, Rita, never fear. We are with you, always near. Close to the river, moon bleed through. We will guide you, guide you through."

DAUGHTER. Mama?

BIG MAMA. I'm here.

DAUGHTER. Mama?

FANNIE MAE. I'm here.

DAUGHTER. Mama?

ALL WOMEN. We here. *(ALL WOMEN circle DAUGHTER as they give gifts and sing. FANNIE MAE dances to DAUGHTER and gives her the sheer silver or white scarf from her waist, then exits. DAUGHTER accepts it and begins upbeat "Yemenjah." WOMEN circle and sing then change to "Yemenjah ah say soo." BIG MAMA gives DAUGHTER her Bible.)*

BIG MAMA. I love you, Daughter. *(ALL WOMEN exit. DAUGHTER comes back to present, removes her scarf. Puts on her hat and coat and takes the basket and other gifts, leaves singing. "Yemenjah ah say soo.")*

DAUGHTER. My Big Mamas had well prepared me for the river. I was blessed to have so many women, so much love. I keep their gifts in my heart, and I know to pass them on.

CURTAIN—END

ADDITIONAL CHARACTER NOTES

BIG MAMA: Very religious. A healer and storyteller. Sings spirituals with feeling.

AUNT MAE: An independent woman. A sensuous sister. Her clothes and jewelry are flashy. She has a wicked laugh and sexy walk.

MISS CORINE: Wears hair in long braid or wrapped.

MAGGIE: Wears long wig or hair piece.

MISS TOM: Married to Miss Lily. Only woman in pants.

MISS LAMAMA: Has affected, distinctly African accent.

MISS ROSA: Very proper gossip, dressed in black, perpetual mourning.

DIRECTOR'S NOTES

DIRECTOR'S NOTES